"The Joy of Christmas: Tips for Maximizing Your Holiday Experience"

Table of Contents

Introduction

Christmas is a time for joy, celebration, and spending quality time with loved ones. It's also a time when we can feel overwhelmed by the demands of the season, from shopping and cooking to entertaining and traveling. In "The Joy of Christmas," readers will learn how to make the most of their holiday experience, from incorporating meaningful traditions and thoughtful gift-giving, to taking care of themselves and creating special memories with their loved ones. With practical tips and inspiration, this book will help readers discover the true joy of Christmas and make it a time to remember.

Chapter 1

The Meaning of Christmas

Christmas is a holiday that is celebrated around the world and holds a variety of meanings for different people. For some, Christmas is a religious holiday that commemorates the birth of Jesus Christ and the values of love, compassion, and forgiveness that he embodies. For others, it is a time to come together with family and friends, exchange gifts, and celebrate the joys of the season. Still others see it as a time of giving back to the community through acts of service or charitable giving.

No matter what Christmas means to you, it is a time to reflect on the things that bring joy and meaning to your life. It is a time to celebrate the love and connection that you have with the people in your life, and to appreciate the many blessings that you have received. It is also a time to be grateful for the things that bring you happiness and fulfillment, whether it is the warmth of loved ones, the beauty of the natural world, or the sense of purpose and accomplishment that comes from meaningful work.

There are many different ways in which people celebrate Christmas, and the holiday holds a variety of meanings for different people. Some people celebrate Christmas as a religious holiday, attending church services, singing carols, and reflecting on the teachings of Jesus Christ. For others, Christmas is a time to come together with family and friends, exchange gifts, and enjoy special meals and activities. Some people celebrate Christmas by decorating their homes with lights, trees, and other festive decorations, while others prefer to travel and experience new traditions and cultures.

In addition to these more traditional forms of celebration, there are also many other ways in which people mark the holiday season. Some people celebrate Christmas by participating in charitable acts or volunteering their time to help others. Others celebrate by embracing the winter season and enjoying outdoor activities like skiing, ice skating, or snowball fights. Still others celebrate by indulging in holiday-themed movies, music, or other forms of entertainment.

No matter how people choose to celebrate Christmas, it is a time for joy, celebration, and connection with loved ones. It is a time to reflect on the things that bring meaning and happiness to our lives, and to appreciate the love and support of those around us. By embracing the diverse ways in which people celebrate Christmas, we can enrich our own holiday experiences and find joy in the many different expressions of this special time of year.

The holiday season is a time for joy, celebration, and connection with loved ones, but it can also be a time of stress and overwhelm. With so many demands on our time and energy, it can be easy to lose sight of the things that bring us joy and meaning. That's why it is so important to take the time to find your own personal sense of meaning and joy during the holiday season. One way to do this is to focus on the things that matter most to you and that bring you happiness and fulfillment. This might include spending time with loved ones, participating in traditions or activities that are meaningful to you, or finding ways to give back to the community. It could also mean taking time for self-care and relaxation, or pursuing hobbies and interests that bring you joy.

Another way to find meaning and joy during the holiday season is to be present and mindful in the moment, rather than stressing about the future or dwelling on the past. This might mean practicing gratitude and finding ways to express appreciation for the people and things in your life, or simply taking time to savor the simple pleasures of the season.

By taking the time to find your own personal sense of meaning and joy during the holiday season, you can make the most of this special time of year and find lasting happiness and fulfillment.

Chapter 2

Creating Meaningful Traditions

There are many different types of traditions that people enjoy during the holiday season. Some people celebrate Christmas, which is a holiday that commemorates the birth of Jesus Christ. This holiday is typically marked by the exchange of gifts, the singing of carols, and the decorating of trees.

Other people celebrate Hanukkah, which is a Jewish holiday that commemorates the miracle of the oil that lasted for eight days in the temple. This holiday is typically marked by the lighting of the menorah, the playing of dreidel games, and the exchange of gifts.

Still others celebrate Kwanzaa, which is an African-American holiday that celebrates the cultural heritage and traditions of the African diaspora. This holiday is typically marked by the lighting of the kinara, the recitation of the principles of Kwanzaa, and the celebration of African music and dance.

In addition to these specific holiday traditions, many people also enjoy more general holiday traditions such as decorating their homes with lights and other decorations, baking cookies and other treats, and spending time with loved ones. No matter what traditions people choose to celebrate, the holiday season is a time for joy, celebration, and coming together with loved ones.

Here are some tips for creating your own meaningful traditions during the holiday season:

Reflect on what matters most to you and your loved ones during the holiday season. This could be spending time together, giving back to the community, or finding ways to relax and de-stress.

Think about what traditions from your past have been most meaningful to you and try to incorporate those into your holiday celebrations.

Consider starting a new tradition that aligns with your values and brings joy to you and your loved ones. This could be something as simple as starting a holiday movie marathon or as elaborate as taking a trip to a new destination.

Don't be afraid to mix and match traditions from different cultures or to put your own twist on existing traditions. This can make the holiday season feel more personal and meaningful.

Involve your loved ones in the process of creating new traditions. This can help to ensure that everyone feels invested in the traditions and make them more meaningful for everyone.

Remember that traditions don't have to be grand or elaborate to be meaningful. Sometimes the simplest traditions can be the most memorable and special.

Overall, the key to creating meaningful traditions during the holiday season is to focus on what matters most to you and your loved ones and to find ways to celebrate and connect with one another in a way that feels authentic and genuine.

Chapter 3

Gift-Giving with a Purpose

Gift-giving is a central part of many holiday celebrations, and it can be a wonderful way to show loved ones that you care. However, it can also be a source of stress and financial strain, especially if you feel pressure to buy the perfect gift or overspend. In this chapter, we will discuss ways to approach gift-giving with intention and purpose, rather than just going through the motions or succumbing to consumerism. Some ideas for thoughtful gift-giving might include:

Giving gifts that are handmade or personal

Giving gifts that are handmade or personal can be a meaningful and thoughtful way to celebrate the holiday season. Here are a few ideas for giving gifts that are handmade or personal:

Make a handmade gift yourself. This could be something as simple as baking cookies or making a piece of art, or something more elaborate like knitting a sweater or building a piece of furniture.

Give a gift that is personal to the recipient. This could be something that holds special meaning for them, like a photograph or a handwritten note, or something that reflects their interests or hobbies.

Consider giving a gift that involves a shared experience, such as tickets to a concert or a gift certificate for a cooking class. This can be a great way to create lasting memories and strengthen bonds with loved ones.

Look for handmade or locally made gifts at artisan markets or small businesses. Supporting local artisans and small businesses can be a great way to give back to your community while also finding unique and meaningful gifts.

A little thought and effort can go a long way in making a gift feel truly special and appreciated.

Giving gifts that are experiential or that create lasting memories

Giving gifts that are experiential or that create lasting memories can be a great way to show your loved ones that you care about them and that you want them to have a meaningful and memorable experience. These types of gifts can range from tickets to a concert or sporting event, to a gift certificate for a cooking class or spa day, to a weekend getaway or vacation.

Experiential gifts allow the recipient to create new memories and have unique and fulfilling experiences, rather than just receiving a tangible object that may eventually be forgotten or discarded. They can also be more personal and meaningful, as they show that you have put thought and effort into finding something that aligns with the interests and passions of the recipient.

Additionally, experiential gifts often allow for shared experiences and create opportunities for bonding and strengthening relationships. For example, if you give a gift of tickets to a play or concert, you can also attend the event together and create a shared memory.

Overall, giving gifts that are experiential or that create lasting memories can be a thoughtful and meaningful way to show your loved ones that you care about them and want them to have enjoyable and memorable experiences.

Giving gifts that are functional or that support a loved one's hobbies or interests

Giving a gift that is functional or supports a loved one's hobbies or interests can be a thoughtful and meaningful gesture. These types of gifts show that you have taken the time to consider the recipient's needs and passions, and that you want to support them in their pursuits. For example, if your friend is an avid baker, you could give them a set of high-quality baking tools or a cookbook featuring their favorite type of cuisine. If your partner is a runner, you could give them a new pair of running shoes or a fitness tracker to help them track their progress. In addition to being practical and useful, these gifts can also be a source of enjoyment and inspiration for the recipient. By choosing a gift that aligns with their interests and hobbies, you are showing your support and appreciation for the things that are important to them.

Giving gifts that are environmentally friendly or that support a cause

During the holiday season, giving gifts that are environmentally friendly or that support a cause can be a meaningful and thoughtful way to show your love and appreciation for your loved ones. These types of gifts not only benefit the recipient, but they also have a positive impact on the world. For example, you could give a gift that is made from sustainable materials, such as a reusable water bottle or a tote bag made from organic cotton. You could also give a gift that supports a cause that is important to you or the recipient, such as a charitable donation or a product that donates a portion of its profits to a specific cause. These types of gifts not only show that you care about the recipient, but they also demonstrate your commitment to making a positive impact on the world. By choosing gifts that are environmentally friendly or that support a cause, you can spread joy and kindness during the holiday season while also making a positive difference in the world.

The importance of setting boundaries around gift-giving

Setting boundaries around gift-giving can be a healthy and practical way to manage your holiday spending and avoid feeling overwhelmed or stressed. Establishing a budget for gift-giving can help you stay within your financial means and avoid overspending, which can lead to financial strain or even debt. You can also consider opting for a secret Santa exchange instead of buying gifts for everyone, which can be a fun and cost-effective way to celebrate the holiday season. In a secret Santa exchange, each participant is randomly assigned to buy a gift for one other person, rather than buying gifts for everyone in the group. This can help to minimize the financial burden of gift-giving and ensure that everyone still has the opportunity to exchange gifts and show their appreciation for one another. By setting boundaries around gift-giving and finding creative ways to celebrate the holiday season, you can avoid feeling overwhelmed or stressed and focus on the joy and meaning of the season.

By approaching gift-giving with purpose and intention, you can make the holiday season more enjoyable and less stressful for yourself and your loved ones.

Chapter 4

Taking Care of Yourself During the Holidays

Taking care of yourself during the holidays is important for maintaining your physical and mental well-being. The holiday season can be a busy and stressful time, with a lot of demands on your time and energy. It is important to make sure you are taking care of your own needs and not overextending yourself. Here are some ways to take care of yourself during the holiday season:

Setting boundaries and saying no to commitments that don't align with your values or goals

Setting boundaries and saying no to commitments that don't align with your values or goals can help you prioritize your time and energy and ensure that you are able to enjoy the holiday season in a way that feels authentic and meaningful to you. It is important to remember that it is okay to say no to invitations or obligations that don't align with your priorities or that you simply don't have the time or energy for. It is also okay to set boundaries around your time and energy and make it clear to others what you are and are not able to do. By setting boundaries and being honest about your limitations, you can protect your own well-being and make sure that you are able to fully participate in the things that are most important to you during the holiday season.

Taking breaks and finding time for relaxation and fun

It's important to remember to take breaks and make time for relaxation and fun, even if you have a lot going on. Here are some tips for finding time for relaxation and fun during the holiday season:

Set aside time for yourself: Make a conscious effort to carve out some time each day or week for yourself. This could be as simple as taking a walk, reading a book, or watching a movie.

Say no to unnecessary commitments: It's okay to decline invitations or requests if they don't fit into your schedule or if you're feeling overwhelmed. Prioritize the things that are most important to you and let go of the rest.

Practice self-care: Take care of your physical and mental health by getting enough sleep, eating well, and engaging in activities that bring you joy and relaxation.

Find ways to de-stress: Consider incorporating stress-reducing activities into your daily routine, such as meditation, yoga, or deep breathing exercises.

Have fun: Don't forget to have fun and enjoy the holiday season. Make time for activities that bring you joy and laughter, whether that's spending time with loved ones, participating in holiday traditions, or trying out new hobbies.

Eating nourishing foods and getting enough sleep

Eating nourishing foods means choosing foods that are high in nutrients and provide our bodies with the energy and fuel they need to function properly. This can include a variety of fruits, vegetables, whole grains, and lean proteins. It is also important to pay attention to portion sizes and try to avoid overeating or consuming too much sugar or unhealthy fats.

Getting enough sleep is also crucial for our overall health and well-being. Aim for 7-9 hours of sleep each night to give your body the rest it needs to repair and regenerate. It can be tempting to stay up late during the holiday season, but try to prioritize getting enough sleep to avoid feeling exhausted or run down. This can help us feel our best and enjoy the holiday season to the fullest.

Practicing gratitude and mindfulness to stay present and focused on the present moment

It can be easy to get caught up in the hustle and bustle and lose sight of what's most important. Practicing gratitude and mindfulness can help us stay present and focused on the present moment, rather than getting caught up in stress and worry.

Here are some tips;

Take a moment each day to reflect on the things you're grateful for: This could be as simple as taking a few minutes to jot down a few things you're thankful for in a journal, or sharing them with a loved one. Focusing on the things you're grateful for can help shift your perspective and bring a sense of calm and contentment.

Pay attention to your senses: Engaging your senses can help bring you into the present moment and away from stress and worries. Take time to savor your food, listen to music, or enjoy the sights and sounds of the holiday season.

Practice mindfulness meditation: Mindfulness meditation involves focusing your attention on the present moment, without judgment. Taking a few minutes each day to sit in stillness and focus on your breath can help you feel more grounded and present.

Be present with others: When you're with loved ones, make an effort to be fully present and engaged in the moment. Turn off your phone and give your full attention to the people you're with.

Seeking support from friends, family, or a professional if you are feeling overwhelmed or distressed.
The holiday season can be a joyful time, but it can also be a difficult and stressful period for many people. If you are feeling overwhelmed or distressed during the holiday season, it is important to remember that you are not alone and there are resources available to help you cope.

By taking care of yourself and prioritizing your own well-being, you can better handle the demands of the holiday season and enjoy it to the fullest.

Chapter 5

Celebrating with Loved Ones

The holiday season is a time to come together with loved ones and create special memories. Whether you are celebrating with a small group of close family and friends or a larger extended family, there are many ways to make the holiday season a time to remember.

Here are a few ideas:

Plan activities together: Consider planning special activities or outings to do with your loved ones. This could be something as simple as going for a walk or as elaborate as planning a day trip.

Connect over shared interests: Take time to engage in activities that you and your loved ones enjoy together. This could be anything from playing board games or watching a movie to cooking a meal or working on a craft project.

Create new traditions: If you are unable to do your usual holiday activities due to certain circumstances, consider creating new traditions to celebrate together. This could be something as simple as starting a new holiday movie marathon or as elaborate as planning a special holiday meal.

Make time for meaningful conversations: The holiday season is a great time to connect with loved ones and have meaningful conversations. Consider setting aside time to talk about what is going on in each other's lives and share your thoughts and feelings.

Show appreciation: Take time to express your appreciation for your loved ones. This could be through thoughtful gestures, such as giving a gift or writing a heartfelt note, or simply telling them how much you appreciate them.

Overall, there are many ways to make the most of your time with loved ones during the holiday season and these also include;
creating traditions or rituals that bring everyone together, such as decorating a tree or cooking a special meal,
playing games or engaging in activities that are fun and interactive,
sharing stories and memories, or creating a time capsule to capture the highlights of the holiday season.
Taking time to reflect on the things that you are grateful for and the love that you have for one another.

By focusing on connection and celebration with your loved ones, you can create lasting memories and make the holiday season a truly special time.

Chapter 6

Embracing the Spirit of the Season

The holiday season is a time of joy, love, and celebration, but it can also be a time when we feel overwhelmed or disconnected from the things that really matter. In this final chapter, we will discuss ways to embrace the spirit of the season and find meaning and joy in the holiday season, no matter what challenges you may be facing. Some ideas for embracing the spirit of the season might include:

Focusing on the things that bring you joy, whether it's a special tradition, a loved one's company, or a sense of accomplishment.Some people find joy in participating in traditional holiday activities, such as decorating the tree or attending a holiday concert. Others may find joy in spending time with loved ones and creating new memories together. For some, a sense of accomplishment can bring joy, whether it's through completing a task or achieving a goal.Whatever brings you joy during the holiday season, it is important to make time for these things and prioritize them in your life. This can help you feel more balanced and centered during a busy time of year.Remember to take a step back and reflect on the things that truly bring you joy during the holiday season. By focusing on these things, you can find a sense of happiness and contentment in the midst of the holiday hustle and bustle.

Being present and mindful in the moment, rather than stressing about the future or dwelling on the past. It can be easy to get caught up in stress and worry about the future or dwelling on the past. However, it is important to try to be present and mindful in the moment, rather than letting these thoughts consume us. Being present and mindful means focusing on the here and now and being aware of our thoughts, feelings, and surroundings. It involves being fully engaged in the activities and people around us, rather than letting our minds wander to other places.

To be present and mindful, try practicing techniques such as mindfulness meditation or deep breathing. These can help you focus your attention on the present moment and let go of any distractions. You can also try setting aside specific times each day to be present and mindful, such as taking a few minutes to sit in silence or focusing on your breath.

Practicing gratitude and finding ways to express appreciation for the people and things in your life

Finding ways to give back to the community or help those in need
Letting go of perfectionism and learning to embrace the imperfections and quirks that make the holiday season special
By embracing the spirit of the season, you can find joy and meaning in the holiday season and make it a time to remember.

Conclusion

This book has provided a wealth of tips and strategies for making the most of the holiday season. From focusing on nourishing foods and getting enough sleep to seeking support from loved ones and being present and mindful, these strategies can help you find joy and happiness during the holiday season.

Remember to take care of yourself and prioritize the things that bring you joy, whether it's participating in traditional holiday activities or creating new memories with loved ones. And don't forget to be present and mindful in the moment, rather than stressing about the future or dwelling on the past.

By following these tips and finding your own unique ways to celebrate the holiday season, you can maximize your holiday experience and create lasting memories. So, embrace the joy of Christmas and have a happy holiday season!

www.ingramcontent.com/pod-product-compliance
Lightning Source LLC
LaVergne TN
LVHW020534160826
845677LV00015B/4060

* 9 7 9 8 3 7 0 5 9 9 1 3 2 *